SCIENTOLOGY
Making the World a Better Place

Founded and developed by L. Ron Hubbard, Scientology is an applied religious philosophy which offers an exact route through which anyone can regain the truth and simplicity of his spiritual self.

Scientology consists of specific axioms that define the underlying causes and principles of existence and a vast area of observations in the humanities, a philosophic body that literally applies to the entirety of life.

This broad body of knowledge resulted in two applications of the subject: first, a technology for man to increase his spiritual awareness and attain the freedom sought by many great philosophic teachings; and, second, a great number of fundamental principles men can use to improve their lives. In fact, in this second application, Scientology offers nothing less than practical methods to better *every* aspect of our existence—means to create new ways of life. And from this comes the subject matter you are about to read.

Compiled from the writings of L. Ron Hubbard, the data presented here is but one of the tools which can be found in *The Scientology Handbook*. A comprehensive guide, the handbook contains numerous applications of Scientology which can be used to improve many other areas of life.

In this booklet, the editors have augmented the data with a short introduction, practical exercises and examples of successful application.

Courses to increase your understanding and further materials to broaden your knowledge are available at your nearest Scientology church or mission, listed at the back of this booklet.

Many new phenomena about man and life are described in Scientology, and so you may encounter terms in these pages you are not familiar with. These are described the first time they appear and in the glossary at the back of the booklet.

Scientology is for use. It is a practical philosophy, something one *does*. Using this data, you *can* change conditions.

Millions of people who want to do something about the conditions they see around them have applied this knowledge. They know that life can be improved. And they know that Scientology works.

Use what you read in these pages to help yourself and others and you will too.

CHURCH OF SCIENTOLOGY INTERNATIONAL

Where once the family was the stable foundation upon which all else was built, today its shattered remnants are the source of much of what troubles society. And while marriages still outnumber divorces, the gap is rapidly closing. Marriage is well on the way to becoming a failed institution.

L. Ron Hubbard wrote extensively on interpersonal relationships and much of it is applicable to this most personal of relationships. In this booklet you will discover methods to make a marriage work, why many marriages fail, how to discover if partners are well suited to each other, and how to save a failing marriage.

While our magazines are filled with the advice of "pop" psychologists, the trend has only worsened. Here are real solutions—workable solutions—that can be applied to improve any intimate relationship.■

WHAT IS MARRIAGE?

When someone begins on that arrangement called marriage, he is getting into something which is, to say the least, adventurous. When a couple get married, they are doing something they know nothing about. And, from all indications, when they have tried it more than once, they know no more about it the second time than they did the first.

Marriage is the foundation of the family unit. In this society and time, the family is the closest knit, self-perpetuating, self-protecting unit. It is necessary economically and otherwise to the society the way it is set up in present time. A culture will go by the boards if its basic building block, the family, is removed as a valid building block. So one can be fairly sure that he who destroys marriage destroys the civilization.

The marriage relationship, basically, is a *postulated* relationship. A *postulate* is a conclusion, decision or resolution about something. When people stop postulating a marriage, it ceases to exist. That is what happens to most marriages. It isn't the other way around. It isn't that all men are evil, so therefore, contracts such as marriage dissolve usually in infidelity and go all to pieces. That is not true. The reverse is true. When you have a purely postulated relationship, you have to continue to create it. And a family which doesn't continue to create itself as a family will cease to exist as a family. That's about all you need to know about it.

A marriage is something which exists primarily because each partner has postulated its existence and its continued existence. Only with this foundation in place are marriages successful.

Where people are having trouble with marriage, it is because they are expecting it to run on automatic. They think it will hang together through no effort of their own; unfortunately, it won't. It has to be created.

Perhaps someone whose parents weren't making too good a go of it, looked at this and decided, "Now, look at that! This institution which is inherent in nature, which nothing will ever change, doesn't perpetuate itself and is not much good because it isn't hanging together."

He had a failure. He probably tried to postulate the family into a unit when he was very young. He was working at it, trying to get a Papa-loves-Mama thing going one way or the other, trying to show them that they had something to live for and so forth.

As a matter of fact, one of the reasons a child gets himself injured is to make his parents realize they have responsibilities for the family. Childhood illness and all this sort of thing occur directly after familial upsets.

Nonetheless, whether an individual had in his own parents a good example of a stable marriage or not, it has nothing to do with whether or not he can make a successful marriage.

If you think that everything else is rigged to perpetuate a marriage while you're not trying to keep it going, of course it will end up in destruction. But if you approach this with the realization that a marriage is something you have to postulate into existence and keep there, and when you stop working at it, it will cease, and if you know the technology contained in the remaining part of this booklet, you can make any marriage stick or you can recover any facet of any marriage, or plaster one back together again any way you want to. But it takes a little doing and it takes a little guts and that is an understatement.

Morals and Transgressions

Whenever people get together and operate as groups, they make agreements, whether actually stated or not, regarding what is right and what is wrong, what is moral and what is immoral—in other words, what will be contributive to survival and what will be destructive of survival. This is a moral code—a series of agreements to which a person has subscribed to guarantee the survival of the group. It doesn't matter what the size of the group is—whether it is a group of two people forming a marriage or a whole nation being formed—they enter into certain agreements.

When one or the other of the partners in a relationship or a marriage transgresses against the agreed-upon moral code, he or she often feels that he cannot tell the other about it. But these transgressions, unspoken but nevertheless transgressions, can gradually mount up and cause a disintegration of the relationship.

In Scientology, a harmful act or a transgression against the mores of the group is called an *overt act* or *overt*. When a person does something that is contrary to the moral code he has agreed to, or when he omits to do something that he *should* have done per that moral code, he has committed an overt act. An overt act violates what was agreed upon.

An unspoken, unannounced transgression against a moral code by which the person is bound is called a *withhold*. A withhold is, then, an overt act that a person committed that he or she is not talking about. Any withhold comes *after* an overt act.

These transgressions are the degree that a person has separated himself from free communication with the remainder of the group. If, for example, a man gambles away the money needed to pay the family bills, he has committed an overt act. And if he then hides this fact and never mentions it to his wife or family, he would be *pretending* to be part of the group while no longer being part of it, as he has broken the agreements that the group is based on. It is this factor which causes the disintegration of a group or a family or a marriage.

A marriage which has broken down into a super-separateness of overt acts and withholds is almost impossible to put back together by just postulating it into existence. After people have separated themselves out from each other, they have to "un-separate" themselves again.

This action is a violation of the agreements of the marriage and is classified as an overt act.

> How was your day, honey?
>
> OK.

The man is reluctant to communicate to his wife what he did. This is an example of a withhold.

Some who get married may think the way this is supposed to go is: on some bright June day this handsome brute (or not so handsome), and this beautiful girl (or not so beautiful), come together, and they say, "I do, till death do us part…" And they think they have now made a marriage. They haven't even started yet.

They have to find out how they look before breakfast. This arrangement has more to do with cosmetics and razor blades than anything else. They have to learn to live with each other if they can. And to some degree, they have wiped out, more or less by the act of getting married, what they were doing before that and they start from there.

What happens from there on out is what counts. But sometimes things they have done before, which they are violently withholding from each other, don't even let the marriage get started and forty-eight hours later their marriage is on the rocks because there is just too much overt and withhold before they even knew each other.

But even that one can be salvaged.

In a marriage which has ground on for years and years, overt acts and withholds can mount up until the partners "grow apart." It's considered to be traditional that at the end of three years, husbands and wives don't get any "kick" out of each other. This is sort of textbook and "all the psychologists know it," but they don't know *why*. It's the overt acts and withholds.

If at the end of three years this is the case, how about at the end of ten? By that time, many couples have just learned to endure. They are both in propitiation—a state of trying to appease each other or reduce the anger of each other. They are getting along somehow and they would rather have it that way than some other way; they would rather be married than not and they think they're making it okay. They don't think too much about the girl or the guy they should have married instead anymore. It's going along somehow.

Now into that relationship we can introduce one of the most startling assaults: we can clear up the marriage!

All a divorce is, or all an inclination or withdrawal is, is simply too many overts and withholds against the marital partner. It's as uncomplicated as that.

When a marital partner is straining and wanting to leave and saying, "I ought to go" or "I ought not to stay" or "I ought to do something else" or "We ought to split up" or "I'd be much better off if we hadn't," all of those rationales stem immediately from the overt acts and withholds of the partner making those rationales against the other partner.

Actually, the basic reason a person does this is that he's trying to protect the other partner from his own viciousness. So he says, "Well, I'd better leave," "We'd better break it up" or "We should cool it off." And that's usually the gradual approach of a marriage breakup—"Cool it off," "I ought to leave," "We should part." But we can take these things now and "uncool" them off.

Probably while you're trying to clean up a marriage between a couple, they will undoubtedly decide that it's all over and there's no reason to go on with it because one couldn't possibly... The thing that saves the day each time is to get each to remember what *he* himself or *she* herself did. If they just keep that thought firmly in mind, it will come through to a perfect completion.

Remedies

One way to alleviate this condition is to have the husband and wife write up their overts on and withholds from their marital partner. Each spouse writes down his overts and withholds on paper, giving the details of the specific time and place the overt/withhold was done, and what was done and/or withheld. When this is fully done, the person can experience relief and a return of responsibility. (This procedure of writing up one's overts and withholds is covered in full in the "Integrity and Honesty" booklet.)

There can be instances where writing up overts and withholds do not fully relieve the discord between the marriage partners. Where this occurs, one should contact a Scientology auditor to help rectify the matter. An auditor is someone who is trained and qualified to apply Scientology processing to individuals for their benefit. Processing is a special form of personal counseling, unique in Scientology, which helps someone view his own existence and which improves his abilities.

Another answer to restore a high level of communication between marital partners is Scientology Marriage Counseling. This is also provided by a Scientology auditor.

A husband and wife can utilize good, honest communication between themselves to create and continue a happy, fulfilling marriage. If both of the people involved work at keeping the agreements they have made and abide by the moral codes, and if the couple keeps the communication free and open between them, they will strengthen their relationship.

Withhold

Withhold

Withhold

Withhold

A withhold is an undisclosed contrasurvival act. If a husband and wife have withholds, the marriage will suffer.

A Scientology auditor can help restore communication between the couple by relieving them of their transgressions.

Communication that is free and open is vital to any lasting and fulfilling relationship.

Communication
in Marriage

There is another key factor in creating a successful marriage, or repairing one that has deteriorated. This also involves communication—the interchange of ideas between two individuals.

Communication is, in fact, the root of marital success from which a strong union can grow. Noncommunication is the rock on which the ship will bash out her keel.

In the first place, men and women aren't too careful "on whom they up and marry." In the absence of any basic training about neurosis, psychosis, or how to judge a good cook or a good wage earner, that tricky, treacherous and not always easy-to-identify thing called "love" is the sole guiding factor in the selection of mates. It is too much to expect of a society above the level of ants to be entirely practical about an institution as basically impractical as marriage. Thus, it is not amazing that the misselection of partners goes on with such abandon.

There are ways, however, not only to select a marriage partner, but also to guarantee the continuation of that marriage; and these ways are simple. They depend uniformly upon communication.

There should be some parity (equality) of intellect and sanity between a husband and wife for them to have a successful marriage. In Western culture, it is expected that the women shall have some command of the humanities (cultural studies such as language, literature, philosophy and art) and sciences. It is easy to establish the educational background of a potential marriage partner; it is not so easy to gauge their capability on the second dynamic or their sanity. (A dynamic is an urge toward existence in an area of life. The second dynamic is the urge toward existence as a future generation. It has two compartments: sex, and the family unit. The "Dynamics of Existence" booklet covers the subject of the dynamics.)

In the past, efforts were made to establish sanity with inkblots, square blocks and tests with marbles to find out if anybody had lost any. The resulting figures had to be personally interpreted with a crystal ball and then reinterpreted for application.

In Scientology, there is a test for sanity and comparative sanity which is so simple that anyone can apply it. What is the "communication lag" of the individual? "Lag" means an interval between events. When asked a question, how long does it take him to answer? When a remark is addressed to him, how long does it take for him to register and return? The elapsed time is what is called the communication lag. The fast answer tells of the fast mind and the sane mind, providing the answer is a sequitur—something following logically; the slow answer tells of less ability and sanity. Marital partners who have the same communication lag will get along; where one partner is fast and one is slow, the situation will become unbearable to the fast partner and miserable to the slow one. Further, Scientology when applied will be more swiftly active in the case of the fast partner and so the imparity under processing will grow beyond either's ability to cope with the matter.

How to process a marriage and keep it a marriage is a problem a large number of auditors would like to have answered. It is not too difficult a problem. One simply takes the slow communication lag member of the team and processes that one first, for this will be the harder, longer case. By speeding up the slow one, parity is neared with the fast communication lag partner, and no objection will be offered. If the fast one is chosen for processing, or if both of them enter processing at the same time, the ratio will not be neared but widened and a marital breach will ensue.

The repair of a marriage which is going on the rocks does not always require the processing of the marriage partners. It may be that another family factor is in the scene. This may be in the person of a relative, such as the mother-in-law. How does one solve this factor? This, again, is simple. The mother-in-law, if there is trouble in the family, may be responsible for cutting communication channels or diverting communication. One or the other of the partners, then, is cut off the communication channel on which he belongs. He senses this and objects strenuously to it.

There is another way of cutting communication which happens when jealousy is involved. It is the largest factor in breaking up marriages. Jealousy comes about because of the insecurity of the jealous person and the jealousy may or may not have foundation. This person is afraid of hidden communication lines and will do anything to try to uncover them. This acts upon the other partner to make him feel that his communication lines are being cut; for he thinks himself entitled to have open communication lines, whereas his marital partner insists that he shut many of them. The resultant rows are violent, as represented by the fact that where jealousy exists in a profession such as acting, insurance companies will not issue policies—the suicide rate is too high.

A person who is jealous has something wrong on the subject of communications and, in selecting the partner to be processed first, the auditor should select the jealous person.

The subject of the application of Scientology to marriage could not be covered in many chapters, but here are given the basic clues to a successful marriage—Communicate!

Assist for a Fight with a Spouse

An "assist" is an action which can be done to alleviate a present time discomfort and help a person recover more rapidly from an accident, illness or upset.

When marital tensions have been left unaddressed and unhandled for some time, they can break out with violence. Severe fights can cause quite an emotional upset for either or both partners, and the threat of loss occasioned by such quarrels can be profound.

Where a fight has occurred between marital partners, the following assist can be used to help handle any resultant emotional trauma of husband and/or wife.

This assist may be done by marital partners on each other after a fight or may be used by another person to help one or both partners.

Procedure

1. Tell the person you are going to help them get over any adverse emotional reaction to the fight.

2. Have the person sit down in a comfortable chair across from you.

3. Say to the person, "Give me places where an angry (husband/wife) would be safe." For example, if you were doing this on a wife, you would say, "Give me places where an angry husband would be safe."

4. Get an answer from the person and acknowledge their answer, with a "Thank you," or "Good," etc.

5. Then say to the person, "Give me places where an angry (husband/wife) would find you safe."

6. Get an answer and acknowledge it.

7. Repeat steps 3–6 over and over again until the person is happy again and has had a realization of some kind—about himself, his spouse, the situation or just life in general.

When this occurs, tell the person "End of assist."

Be certain not to evaluate the person's answers for him or tell him how he should answer or what he should think about the situation. Do not berate the person for his answers. This is destructive and can halt all potential gain from the assist.

This assist is not a handling for the situation which *caused* the conflict or discord. Once the immediate upset is under control, the reasons for the fight should be ascertained. For instance, another party such as a relative or associate of a spouse may be creating friction between the marital partners. When this third party, usually hidden, is exposed as the source of the conflict, it resolves. This would be looked into and handled with the techniques covered in the "How to Resolve Conflicts" booklet. Whatever the cause of the difficulty, a full handling for it should be worked out and implemented.

The effects of a fight with a spouse can linger long after the spat itself is over.

Two simple questions, in this case, "Give me places where an angry husband would be safe" and "Give me places where an angry husband would find you safe" can assist a person to free her attention from it.

The questions are asked and answered again and again …

… and can help the person recover from any adverse emotional reaction to the fight.

MAINTAINING A MARRIAGE

A fulfilling marriage has, as an essential ingredient, a high level of communication between the marital partners. When the relationship becomes strained, if they get the overts and withholds off on the marriage, it will be put back together again.

One shouldn't believe that it will go together without a few flying frying pans—you would be a perfectionist if you believed that was going to happen. And don't believe you can all put it together again in one night because the number of overts and withholds can take a little longer to detail.

A marriage can exist but not without two-way communication. And it cannot exist unless it continues to be postulated into existence by the parties involved. If we do these things, we have a marriage.

Marriage, then, would consist of putting together an association between people without overt acts and withholds, postulated into existence and continued for the mutual perpetuation and protection of the members and the group.

It is a very simple arrangement, actually, and a highly satisfactory arrangement if it continues to be simple, but a very complex arrangement if it doesn't continue to be.

It isn't that mothers-in-law are the people who always wreck marriages. You could say offhand that mothers-in-law should all be shot and so forth, and then we would have free marriages and it'd be nice. Or we could have woman's suffrage (their right to vote) and then marriage would be okay, or that we could have complete emancipation, instantaneous divorce, and marriage could be okay.

All of these social, sticky-plaster pieces of nonsense are just efforts to have a marriage without ever really having a marriage. None of these things ever made a marriage—quick divorce or preventing this or that.

The Chinese go the opposite—a marriage occurs but it really doesn't occur because the oldest man of the husband's family is still the head of the family, and the wife still serves the husband's mother, and it all gets very complicated.

We get surrounded by bunches of rules and that sort of thing. We don't care what rules they're surrounded by as long as there is free communication amongst the members of that family—that group. And if there's free communication amongst the members of that group, their affinity is sufficiently high to take the shocks and hammers and pounds of life, and life does hand out a few hammers and pounds and shocks now and again.

If the individuals connected with a family are not self-supportive, then these shocks can be rough one way or the other. The person does something and apparently thinks things are done to him, and he's trying to make it and can't. But on a self-supportive, mutually co-supportive basis, people have a better chance of making it than alone. And that's one of the basic philosophies on which marriage is based.

Of course, a little kid wouldn't make it at all, and none of us would have made it at all, if it hadn't have been for a marriage. The biological pattern of familial relationships and growth is the thing which will carry mankind on.

But a marriage can exist. A marriage, no matter how strained, can be put back together again.■

Practical Exercises

Here are exercises relating to marriage. Doing these exercises will help increase your understanding of what marriage is made up of and how a marriage can be improved.

1 Think of a married couple you know and determine what they are doing to create their marriage. Are they both working to keep the marriage created, or is one or the other or both doing less than they should? Think of or directly observe other married couples you know, and estimate how much the partners are doing to create the marriage, until it is very real to you that a marriage is something that is created.

2 Think of some situation you have seen or experienced where someone continued to create something and later ceased to create it.

3 Find someone who is having some kind of marital difficulty and help him or her by having the person read at least some of the data contained in this booklet.

4 Determine the communication lag of someone. Approach another person and ask him a simple question such as, "How many doors are there in this room?" or "What is the date?" Note how long it takes the person to answer the question you asked. From this determine whether the person has a long or short communication lag.

RESULTS FROM APPLICATION

People recognize that a happy marriage and family form a stable building block of society, despite invitations to follow the "modern" philosophy that divorces and single-parent families are inevitable, and marriage "doesn't work." The technology of Scientology is used by thousands to create and maintain successful marriages or to salvage them where they have gone off the rails. In a broad survey of Scientologists, none (0 percent) thought marriage as a state was undesirable and 91.2 percent thought it vital or desirable. Scientology marriages are not only successful, they are productive of stable family units. Only 2.8 percent of all Scientology married couples have no children, whereas in the United States, for example, 49 percent of all married couples have no children. Yet if you were to question an even apparently cynical person about the workability or desirability of marriage, you would probably find that the person does desire a happy marriage and that past failures, either experienced or observed, have buried the desire. Certainly, the following testimonies would seem to bear this out:

Two people were having extreme marital difficulties. The husband had absolutely decided to end the marriage and was already in the process of dividing their belongings. A Scientologist was asked by the wife to counsel them. This was the result:

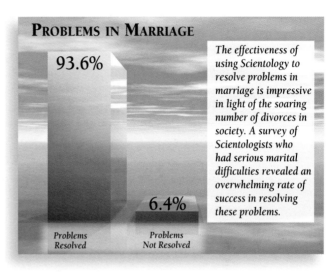

PROBLEMS IN MARRIAGE

93.6%

6.4%

Problems Resolved

Problems Not Resolved

The effectiveness of using Scientology to resolve problems in marriage is impressive in light of the soaring number of divorces in society. A survey of Scientologists who had serious marital difficulties revealed an overwhelming rate of success in resolving these problems.

"The wife really wanted to salvage their marriage but her husband didn't, although he did grudgingly agree to go through the counseling. When I first started counseling them, he was doing this as a mere 'formality.' But after a number of hours of counseling, this situation did a 180-degree turnaround and their marriage was salvaged. They were both very much in love again and were spared the trauma that accompanies divorce."

Nothing had worked for a couple from New York who were trying to save their marriage, so they agreed to separate. A friend sent them to a chaplain in a Scientology church for counseling and when that was complete the wife was overjoyed.

"Well, what can I say! I feel wonderful about myself and about my husband. Two weeks ago I couldn't see how we could stay together. Step by step, each of us took responsibility for ourselves. Then we began to take responsibility for each other. We used to be in very good communication before we drifted apart, but since we completed this counseling, we finish each other's sentences and the same thing comes out of our mouths at the same time! We are both now new people. I owe my life 1,000 times over to the chaplain."

Study of some of Mr. Hubbard's writings on the subject of marriage helped a couple in Los Angeles improve their marriage.

"Each time we learned something new, one or the other of us would apply it. We found that we became a lot more positive in our communication with each other. As we learned more, it was like an adventure—every day of our marriage was something to look forward to, something very exciting, something we created each day. Frankly it had never been that good before. This was just from reading about it. We found each other again—and ourselves."

Through applying the technology of overts and withholds, a young woman from Santa Barbara, California, was able to salvage the marriage of her parents.

"My mother and stepfather were upset with one another and each was telling me bad things about the other. Although I was relatively new to Scientology at that time, one of the things I had learned from Scientology courses was the subject of harmful actions and what causes these and that man, as a being, was basically good.

"Having seen my mother leave one marriage and her second marriage, which started out brilliantly, begin to crumble, I decided to do something about it. I went over a few basics of communication with my parents, and the fact that the basic personality is basically good. I showed them what happens to a person when they commit harmful actions and the results and what makes a person critical about someone as well. They both listened in silence and then I went over the fact that in the beginning of their marriage they had told each other everything and were in very good communication—and how to restore that. When I was sure they fully understood I said that they could apply that to their marriage.

"After that, neither have said a critical thing about the other in the last thirteen years and they are still very much in love. Now they both communicate their love to me and each other and we have a very strong respect for each other."

Disclosing each other's overts and withholds was a matter of course to a Los

Angeles married couple who are Scientologists. Talking about this, the husband said:

"Since we get off overts and with-holds to each other as a basic action of keeping our marriage going well, we listen to each other. This is such a simple thing, but because of it, our marriage continues to flourish."

A couple in Orange County, California, who had not been getting along at all well together, applied the data in this booklet. The woman said:

"This is the best thing that ever happened in our marriage. I have so much love for my husband—more than ever before. It's the first time that I have been able to tell anyone anything and feel it's okay. There is so much more trust. There was so much unfinished communication that is now finished. Now I know that if anything comes up, our communication can handle it."

In Melbourne, Australia, a married couple were fighting chronically, so much so that even their children couldn't escape the unhappiness of their marriage. They were able to handle this situation using Mr. Hubbard's technology of handling overts and withholds.

*"I feel greatly relieved of past upsets and am in very good communication with my husband. The ridding of overts and withholds, no matter how big or small, brings back so much affinity, reality and communication. I can talk to my husband about anything and find that I have a lot more to say and have even broadened my communication to new topics not talked about before. The blow-ups are no longer there; if there is an issue, it is discussed calmly. The children no longer have their ears dunned and their communication has really come up too. **Anyone** who is having marriage trouble and can't communicate **must must** apply the technology of handling overts and withholds. I feel quite 'new' again spiritually, and heaps more happy."*

Despite a sincere wish to have a marriage that would last a lifetime, a young woman had already been divorced twice.

*"I have been married three times. Before I found Mr. Hubbard's discoveries on marriage, I thought I was destined to go from marriage to marriage looking for the 'perfect' man. Boy, was I wrong about this! I have been married to my husband for seven years and because I now know **why** I 'could never be happy with' my earlier husbands, and because I have the tools now to be **really** happy, I know this marriage is for the rest of our lives."*

Separation and divorce sometimes seem to be the only logical solution to marital troubles. Addressing the mechanism of overts and withholds can bring about a true solution to a rocky relationship.

"Before the Scientology marriage counseling I was absolutely sure I wanted out! I would find myself thinking about things I would do and how my life would be without my husband. The counseling was like a kind of magic. I feel now that I can communicate my true feelings to my husband, and my caring for him as a partner has come back. If I had gotten out like I was so sure I wanted to, I would have wasted a beautiful life with a fine man."

A couple whose relationship wasn't in any particular trouble decided to get Scientology marriage counseling purely to improve their marriage. This is what the husband said on completing the counseling:

"It was very good to clear up the communication between my wife and myself. We are in very high affinity, reality and communication with each other now, able to communicate on any subject. This counseling is not just for those on the verge of divorce, but for any couple whose marriage has room for improvement. The counseling works."

A woman from Phoenix had this to say about the rescue of her marriage through the use of Mr. Hubbard's technology:

"About two years into our marriage my husband and I were talking about divorce. The tension and upset got so bad that we could hardly stand sleeping next to each other and nearly every comment either of us would make was taken wrongly by the other. It was utter agony because I loved him very much; each new upset was like a stab in the heart.

"Well, I knew I wasn't going to divorce him so the only way out was to get Scientology marriage counseling. We got together with a chaplain and in about an hour and a half we had found the root of the problem. It took some work after that to get our relationship back to a good, stable state, but now it's terrific. There may be an upset here or a bit of a down moment there but these aren't disasters—we just handle them! Simple but powerful."

A Swiss couple discovered through Scientology the importance of continued creation of a marriage using communication:

*"I had two other relationships before I got married and both were not very successful. It was a big game for me to get in communication with a man, get to know him and start a relationship—but then I would stop **creating** the relationship. I thought that I had accomplished what I wanted, so I didn't do anything further. Both of these relationships ended shortly after they were started, because it became boring and we didn't have anything to say to each other anymore.*

"Then I started to apply Scientology technology on communication and on how to maintain a marriage. I realized that a marriage is like a ship one has to care for and create all the time. I have now been married for more than two years and our marriage is not boring at all. On the contrary, in creating our relationship and in communicating about everything that comes up, we are making our relationship stronger and stronger every day and this game is much more interesting and adventurous than the game I was playing before."

Communication is the root of marital success, from which a strong union can grow. All too often a marriage starts to come apart soon after it begins. Reversing this trend, a Greek woman discovered the value of Scientology training on the skills of communication in creating a rewarding relationship.

"Having learned the basics of communication I now find it completely effortless to communicate with anybody exactly the concept I have in mind. In my marriage I have realized this is extremely helpful as I don't get into any arguments whatsoever; rather I get in communication with my husband very analytically and problems just get solved in a matter of a few minutes. I have a very happy marriage and our love for each other increases more and more as time goes by. Much different from what I have often seen happening with people who do not know and use Scientology technology.

ABOUT
L. RON HUBBARD

No more fitting statement typifies the life of L. Ron Hubbard than his simple declaration: "I like to help others and count it as my greatest pleasure in life to see a person free himself from the shadows which darken his days." Behind these pivotal words stands a lifetime of service to mankind and a legacy of wisdom that enables anyone to attain long-cherished dreams of happiness and spiritual freedom.

Born in Tilden, Nebraska on March 13, 1911, his road of discovery and dedication to his fellows began at an early age. "I wanted other people to be happy, and could not understand why they weren't," he wrote of his youth; and therein lay the sentiments that would long guide his steps. By the age of nineteen, he had traveled more than a quarter of a million miles, examining the cultures of Java, Japan, India and the Philippines.

Returning to the United States in 1929, Ron resumed his formal education and studied mathematics, engineering and the then new field of nuclear physics—all providing vital tools for continued research. To finance that research, Ron embarked upon a literary career in the early 1930s, and soon became one of the most widely read authors of popular fiction. Yet never losing sight of his primary goal, he continued his mainline research through extensive travel and expeditions.

With the advent of World War II, he entered the United States Navy as a lieutenant (junior grade) and served as commander of antisubmarine corvettes. Left partially blind and lame from injuries sustained during combat, he was diagnosed as permanently disabled by 1945. Through application of his theories on the mind, however, he was not only able to help fellow servicemen, but also to regain his own health.

After five more years of intensive research, Ron's discoveries were presented to the world in *Dianetics: The Modern Science of Mental Health*. The first popular handbook on the human mind expressly written for the man in the street, *Dianetics* ushered in a new era of hope for mankind and a new

phase of life for its author. He did, however, not cease his research, and as breakthrough after breakthrough was carefully codified through late 1951, the applied religious philosophy of Scientology was born.

Because Scientology explains the whole of life, there is no aspect of man's existence that L. Ron Hubbard's subsequent work did not address. Residing variously in the United States and England, his continued research brought forth solutions to such social ills as declining educational standards and pandemic drug abuse.

All told, L. Ron Hubbard's works on Scientology and Dianetics total forty million words of recorded lectures, books and writings. Together, these constitute the legacy of a lifetime that ended on January 24, 1986. Yet the passing of L. Ron Hubbard in no way constituted an end; for with a hundred million of his books in circulation and millions of people daily applying his technologies for betterment, it can truly be said the world still has no greater friend.■

GLOSSARY

acknowledge: give (someone) an acknowledgment. *See also* **acknowledgment** in this glossary.

acknowledgment: something said or done to inform another that his statement or action has been noted, understood and received.

affinity: love, liking or any other emotional attitude; the degree of liking. The basic definition of affinity is the consideration of distance, whether good or bad.

assist: a process which can be done to alleviate a present time discomfort and help a person recover more rapidly from an accident, illness or upset.

auditor: someone who is trained and qualified to apply Scientology processing to individuals for their benefit. The term comes from the Latin *audire,* "to listen." *See also* **processing** in this glossary.

communication: an interchange of ideas across space between two individuals.

communication lag: the length of time intervening between the asking of a question and the reply to that specific question by the person asked.

communication line: the route along which a communication travels from one person to another.

dynamic: an urge to survive along a certain course; an urge toward existence in an area of life. There are eight dynamics: first, self; second, sex and the family unit; third, groups; fourth, mankind; fifth, life forms; sixth, physical universe; seventh, spirits; and eighth, Supreme Being.

overt act: a harmful act or a transgression against the moral code of a group. An overt act is not just injuring someone or some-

thing, it is an act of *omission* or *commission* which does the least good for the least number of people or areas of life, or the most harm to the greatest number of people or areas of life.

postulate: (1) (*noun*) a conclusion, decision or resolution about something. (2) (*verb*) make something happen or bring something into being by making a postulate about it.

present time: the time which is now and becomes the past as rapidly as it is observed. It is a term loosely applied to the environment existing in now.

processing: a special form of personal counseling, unique in Scientology, which helps an individual look at his own existence and improves his ability to confront what he is and where he is. Processing is a precise, thoroughly codified activity with exact procedures.

Scientology: an applied religious philosophy developed by L. Ron Hubbard. It is the study and handling of the spirit in relationship to itself, universes and other life. The word *Scientology* comes from the Latin *scio,* which means "know" and the Greek word *logos,* meaning "the word or outward form by which the inward thought is expressed and made known." Thus, Scientology means knowing about knowing.

third party: one who by false reports creates trouble between two people, a person and a group, or a group and another group.

withhold: an unspoken, unannounced transgression against a moral code by which a person is bound; an overt act that a person committed that he or she is not talking about. Any withhold comes *after* an overt act.

CHURCHES OF SCIENTOLOGY

Contact Your Nearest Church or Organization or visit www.volunteerministers.org

UNITED STATES

ALBUQUERQUE

Church of Scientology
8106 Menaul Boulevard NE
Albuquerque, New Mexico 87110

ANN ARBOR

Church of Scientology
66 E. Michigan Avenue
Battle Creek, Michigan 49017

ATLANTA

Church of Scientology
1611 Mt. Vernon Road
Dunwoody, Georgia 30338

AUSTIN

Church of Scientology
2200 Guadalupe
Austin, Texas 78705

BOSTON

Church of Scientology
448 Beacon Street
Boston, Massachusetts 02115

BUFFALO

Church of Scientology
47 West Huron Street
Buffalo, New York 14202

CHICAGO

Church of Scientology
3011 North Lincoln Avenue
Chicago, Illinois 60657-4207

CINCINNATI

Church of Scientology
215 West 4th Street, 5th Floor
Cincinnati, Ohio 45202-2670

CLEARWATER

Church of Scientology
Flag Service Organization
210 South Fort Harrison Avenue
Clearwater, Florida 33756

Foundation Church of
Scientology
Flag Ship Service Organization
c/o *Freewinds* Relay Office
118 North Fort Harrison Avenue
Clearwater, Florida 33755-4013

COLUMBUS

Church of Scientology
30 North High Street
Columbus, Ohio 43215

DALLAS

Church of Scientology
Celebrity Centre Dallas
1850 North Buckner Boulevard
Dallas, Texas 75228

DENVER

Church of Scientology
3385 South Bannock Street
Englewood, Colorado 80110

DETROIT

Church of Scientology
28000 Middlebelt Road
Farmington Hills, Michigan
48334

HONOLULU

Church of Scientology
1146 Bethel Street
Honolulu, Hawaii 96813

KANSAS CITY

Church of Scientology
3619 Broadway
Kansas City, Missouri 64111

LAS VEGAS

Church of Scientology
846 East Sahara Avenue
Las Vegas, Nevada 89104

Church of Scientology
Celebrity Centre Las Vegas
4850 W. Flamingo Road, Ste. 10
Las Vegas, Nevada 89103

LONG ISLAND

Church of Scientology
99 Railroad Station Plaza
Hicksville, New York 11801-2850

LOS ANGELES AND VICINITY

Church of Scientology
of Los Angeles
4810 Sunset Boulevard
Los Angeles, California 90027

Church of Scientology
1451 Irvine Boulevard
Tustin, California 92680

Church of Scientology
1277 East Colorado Boulevard
Pasadena, California 91106

Church of Scientology
15643 Sherman Way
Van Nuys, California 91406

Church of Scientology
American Saint Hill
Organization
1413 L. Ron Hubbard Way
Los Angeles, California 90027

Church of Scientology
American Saint Hill Foundation
1413 L. Ron Hubbard Way
Los Angeles, California 90027

Church of Scientology
Advanced Organization
of Los Angeles
1306 L. Ron Hubbard Way
Los Angeles, California 90027

Church of Scientology
Celebrity Centre International
5930 Franklin Avenue
Hollywood, California 90028

LOS GATOS

Church of Scientology
2155 South Bascom Avenue,
Suite 120
Campbell, California 95008

MIAMI

Church of Scientology
120 Giralda Avenue
Coral Gables, Florida 33134

MINNEAPOLIS

Church of Scientology
Twin Cities
1011 Nicollet Mall
Minneapolis, Minnesota 55403

MOUNTAIN VIEW

Church of Scientology
2483 Old Middlefield Way
Mountain View, California 94043

NASHVILLE

Church of Scientology
Celebrity Centre Nashville
1204 16th Avenue South
Nashville, Tennessee 37212

NEW HAVEN

Church of Scientology
909 Whalley Avenue
New Haven, Connecticut
06515-1728

NEW YORK CITY

Church of Scientology
227 West 46th Street
New York, New York 10036-1409

Church of Scientology
Celebrity Centre New York
65 East 82nd Street
New York, New York 10028

ORLANDO

Church of Scientology
1830 East Colonial Drive
Orlando, Florida 32803-4729

PHILADELPHIA

Church of Scientology
1315 Race Street
Philadelphia, Pennsylvania 19107

PHOENIX
Church of Scientology
2111 West University Drive
Mesa, Arizona 85201

PORTLAND
Church of Scientology
2636 NE Sandy Boulevard
Portland, Oregon 97232-2342
Church of Scientology
Celebrity Centre Portland
708 SW Salmon Street
Portland, Oregon 97205

SACRAMENTO
Church of Scientology
825 15th Street
Sacramento, California
95814-2096

SALT LAKE CITY
Church of Scientology
1931 South 1100 East
Salt Lake City, Utah 84106

SAN DIEGO
Church of Scientology
1330 4th Avenue
San Diego, California 92101

SAN FRANCISCO
Church of Scientology
83 McAllister Street
San Francisco, California 94102

SAN JOSE
Church of Scientology
80 East Rosemary Street
San Jose, California 95112

SANTA BARBARA
Church of Scientology
524 State Street
Santa Barbara, California 93101

SEATTLE
Church of Scientology
2226 3rd Avenue
Seattle, Washington 98121

ST. LOUIS
Church of Scientology
6901 Delmar Boulevard
University City, Missouri 63130

TAMPA
Church of Scientology
3617 Henderson Boulevard
Tampa, Florida 33609-4501

WASHINGTON, DC
Founding Church of Scientology
of Washington, DC
1701 20th Street NW
Washington, DC 20009

PUERTO RICO

HATO REY
Dianetics Center of Puerto Rico
272 JT Piñero Avenue
Hyde Park
San Juan, Puerto Rico 00918

CANADA

EDMONTON
Church of Scientology
10206 106th Street NW
Edmonton, Alberta
Canada T5J 1H7

KITCHENER
Church of Scientology
104 King Street West, 2nd Floor
Kitchener, Ontario
Canada N2G 1A6

MONTREAL
Church of Scientology
4489 Papineau Street
Montreal, Quebec
Canada H2H 1T7

OTTAWA
Church of Scientology
150 Rideau Street, 2nd Floor
Ottawa, Ontario
Canada K1N 5X6

QUEBEC
Church of Scientology
350 Bd Chareste Est
Quebec, Quebec
Canada G1K 3H5

TORONTO
Church of Scientology
696 Yonge Street, 2nd Floor
Toronto, Ontario
Canada M4Y 2A7

VANCOUVER
Church of Scientology
401 West Hastings Street
Vancouver, British Columbia
Canada V6B 1L5

WINNIPEG
Church of Scientology
315 Garry Street, Suite 210
Winnipeg, Manitoba
Canada R3B 2G7

UNITED KINGDOM

BIRMINGHAM
Church of Scientology
8 Ethel Street
Winston Churchill House
Birmingham, England B2 4BG

BRIGHTON
Church of Scientology
Third Floor, 79-83 North Street
Brighton, Sussex
England BN1 1ZA

EAST GRINSTEAD
Church of Scientology
Saint Hill Foundation
Saint Hill Manor
East Grinstead, West Sussex
England RH19 4JY

Advanced Organization
Saint Hill
Saint Hill Manor
East Grinstead, West Sussex
England RH19 4JY

EDINBURGH
Hubbard Academy of Personal
Independence
20 Southbridge
Edinburgh, Scotland EH1 1LL

LONDON
Church of Scientology
68 Tottenham Court Road
London, England W1P 0BB

Church of Scientology
Celebrity Centre London
42 Leinster Gardens
London, England W2 3AN

MANCHESTER
Church of Scientology
258 Deansgate
Manchester, England M3 4BG

PLYMOUTH
Church of Scientology
41 Ebrington Street
Plymouth, Devon
England PL4 9AA

SUNDERLAND
Church of Scientology
51 Fawcett Street
Sunderland, Tyne and Wear
England SR1 1RS

AUSTRALIA

ADELAIDE
Church of Scientology
24-28 Waymouth Street
Adelaide, South Australia
Australia 5000

BRISBANE
Church of Scientology
106 Edward Street, 2nd Floor
Brisbane, Queensland
Australia 4000

CANBERRA
Church of Scientology
43-45 East Row
Canberra City, ACT
Australia 2601

MELBOURNE
Church of Scientology
42-44 Russell Street
Melbourne, Victoria
Australia 3000

PERTH
Church of Scientology
108 Murray Street, 1st Floor
Perth, Western Australia
Australia 6000

SYDNEY
Church of Scientology
201 Castlereagh Street
Sydney, New South Wales
Australia 2000

Church of Scientology
Advanced Organization
Saint Hill Australia,
New Zealand and Oceania
19-37 Greek Street
Glebe, New South Wales
Australia 2037

NEW ZEALAND

AUCKLAND
Church of Scientology
159 Queen Street, 3rd Floor
Auckland 1, New Zealand

AFRICA

BULAWAYO

Church of Scientology
Southampton House, Suite 202
Main Street and 9th Avenue
Bulawayo, Zimbabwe

CAPE TOWN

Church of Scientology
Ground Floor, Dorlane House
39 Roeland Street
Cape Town 8001, South Africa

DURBAN

Church of Scientology
20 Buckingham Terrace
Westville, Durban 3630
South Africa

HARARE

Church of Scientology
404–409 Pockets Building
50 Jason Moyo Avenue
Harare, Zimbabwe

JOHANNESBURG

Church of Scientology
4th Floor, Budget House
130 Main Street
Johannesburg 2001
South Africa

Church of Scientology
No. 108 1st Floor,
   Bordeaux Centre
Gordon Road, Corner Jan
   Smuts Avenue
Blairgowrie, Randburg 2125
South Africa

PORT ELIZABETH

Church of Scientology
2 St. Christopher's
27 Westbourne Road Central
Port Elizabeth 6001
South Africa

PRETORIA

Church of Scientology
307 Ancore Building
Corner Jeppe and Esselen Streets
Sunnyside, Pretoria 0002
South Africa

SCIENTOLOGY MISSIONS

INTERNATIONAL OFFICE

Scientology Missions
   International
6331 Hollywood Boulevard
Suite 501
Los Angeles, California
90028-6314

UNITED STATES

Scientology Missions
   International
Western United States Office
1308 L. Ron Hubbard Way
Los Angeles, California 90027

Scientology Missions
   International
Eastern United States Office
349 W. 48th Street
New York, New York 10036

Scientology Missions
   International
Flag Land Base Office
210 South Fort Harrison Avenue
Clearwater, Florida 33756

AFRICA

Scientology Missions
   International
African Office
6th Floor, Budget House
130 Main Street
Johannesburg 2001, South Africa

AUSTRALIA, NEW ZEALAND AND OCEANIA

Scientology Missions
   International
Australian, New Zealand
and Oceanian Office
201 Castlereagh Street, 3rd Floor
Sydney, New South Wales
Australia 2000

CANADA

Scientology Missions
   International
Canadian Office
696 Yonge Street, 2nd Floor
Toronto, Ontario
Canada M4Y 2A7

UNITED KINGDOM

Scientology Missions
   International
United Kingdom Office
Saint Hill Manor
East Grinstead, West Sussex
England RH19 4JY

TO OBTAIN ANY BOOKS OR CASSETTES BY L. RON HUBBARD WHICH ARE NOT AVAILABLE AT YOUR LOCAL ORGANIZATION, CONTACT ANY OF THE FOLLOWING PUBLICATIONS ORGANIZATIONS WORLDWIDE:

BRIDGE PUBLICATIONS, INC.

4751 Fountain Avenue
Los Angeles, California 90029

www.bridgepub.com

CONTINENTAL PUBLICATIONS LIAISON OFFICE

696 Yonge Street
Toronto, Ontario
Canada M4Y 2A7

NEW ERA PUBLICATIONS INTERNATIONAL ApS

Store Kongensgade 53
1264 Copenhagen K
Denmark

www.newerapublications.com

ERA DINÁMICA EDITORES, S.A. DE C.V.

Pablo Ucello #16
Colonia C.D. de los Deportes
Mexico, D.F.

NEW ERA PUBLICATIONS UK LTD.

Saint Hill Manor
East Grinstead, West Sussex
England RH19 4JY

NEW ERA PUBLICATIONS AUSTRALIA PTY LTD.

Level 1, 61–65 Wentworth
   Avenue
Surry Hills, New South Wales
Australia 2000

CONTINENTAL PUBLICATIONS PTY LTD.

6th Floor, Budget House
130 Main Street
Johannesburg 2001
South Africa

NEW ERA PUBLICATIONS ITALIA S.R.L.

Via Cadorna, 61
20090 Vimodrone (MI), Italy

NEW ERA PUBLICATIONS DEUTSCHLAND GMBH

Hittfelder Kirchweg 5A
21220 Seevetal-Maschen
Germany

NEW ERA PUBLICATIONS FRANCE E.U.R.L.

14, rue des Moulins
75001 Paris, France

NUEVA ERA DINÁMICA, S.A.

C/ Montera 20, 1° dcha.
28013 Madrid, Spain

NEW ERA PUBLICATIONS JAPAN, INC.

Sakai SS bldg 2F, 4-38-15
Higashi-Ikebukuro
Toshima-ku, Tokyo, Japan
170-0013

NEW ERA PUBLICATIONS GROUP

Str. Kasatkina, 16, Building 1
129301 Moscow, Russia

NEW ERA PUBLICATIONS CENTRAL EUROPEAN OFFICE

1438 Budapest
Pf. 351
Hungary

BUILD A BETTER WORLD

BECOME A VOLUNTEER MINISTER

Help bring happiness, purpose and truth to your fellow man.
Become a Volunteer Minister.

Thousands of Volunteer Ministers bring relief and sanity to others all over the world using techniques like the ones found in this booklet. But more help is needed. Your help.

As a Volunteer Minister you can today handle things which seemed impossible yesterday. And you can vastly improve this world's tomorrow.

Become a Volunteer Minister and brighten the world to a better place for you to live.

It's easy to do. For help and information about becoming a Volunteer Minister, visit our website today. www.volunteerministers.org

You can also call or write your nearest Volunteer Ministers International organization.

VOLUNTEER MINISTERS INTERNATIONAL
A DEPARTMENT OF THE INTERNATIONAL HUBBARD ECCLESIASTICAL LEAGUE OF PASTORS

INTERNATIONAL OFFICE
6331 Hollywood Boulevard, Suite 708
Los Angeles, California 90028
Tel: (323) 960-3560 (800) 435-7498

WESTERN US
1308 L. Ron Hubbard Way
Los Angeles, California 90027
Tel: (323) 953-3357
1-888-443-5760
ihelpwestus@earthlink.net

EASTERN US
349 W. 48th Street
New York, New York 10036
Tel: (212) 757-9610
1-888-443-5788

CANADA
696 Yonge Street
Toronto, Ontario
Canada M4Y 2A7
Tel: (416) 968-0070

LATIN AMERICA
Federación Mexicana de
   Dianética, A.C.
Puebla #31
Colonia Roma, CP 06700
Mexico, D.F.
Tel: 525-511-4452

EUROPE
Store Kongensgade 55
1264 Copenhagen K
Denmark
Tel: 45-33-737-322

ITALY
Via Cadorna, 61
20090 Vimodrone (MI)
Italy
Tel: 39-0227-409-246

AUSTRALIA
201 Castlereagh Street
3rd Floor
Sydney, New South Wales
Australia 2000
Tel: 612-9267-6422

AFRICA
6th Floor, Budget House
130 Main Street
Johannesburg 2001
South Africa
Tel: 083-331-7170

UNITED KINGDOM
Saint Hill Manor
East Grinstead, West Sussex
England RH19 4JY
Tel: 44-1342-301-895

HUNGARY
1438 Budapest
PO Box 351, Hungary
Tel: 361-321-5298

**COMMONWEALTH OF
INDEPENDENT
STATES**
c/o Hubbard Humanitarian
   Center
Ul. Borisa Galushkina 19A
129301 Moscow, Russia
Tel: 7-095-961-3414

TAIWAN
2F, 65, Sec. 4
Ming-Sheng East Road
Taipei, Taiwan ROC
Tel: 88-628-770-5074

www.volunteerministers.org

Bridge Publications, Inc.
4751 Fountain Avenue, Los Angeles, CA 90029
ISBN 0-88404-920-5

An L. RON HUBBARD Publication